Tallulah
TUMOUR
friend or foe?

A PERSONAL INSIGHT INTO A
BATTLE WITH A BRAIN TUMOUR

FIONA GOLDSBY

Tallulah
TUMOUR
friend or foe?

MEMOIRS

Cirencester

WE ARE
MACMILLAN.
CANCER SUPPORT

All profits derived from the sale of this book will be donated to Macmillan Cancer Support, registered charity number 261017.

Published by Memoirs

MEMOIRS
PUBLISHING

25 Market Place, Cirencester, Gloucestershire, GL7 2NX
info@memoirsbooks.co.uk www.memoirspublishing.com

Printed in England

Foreword

This book is designed to help others dealing with the diagnosis of a brain tumour. It is intended to provide information about what you may expect, with hints and tips to deal with the side effects.

When I was going along my journey there was very little information available, given that it is a fairly rare condition, and I found I had to ask. I hope this publication will give you ideas on what questions to ask.

The information in the book will not only be helpful to patients, but to caregivers and family members. While you will encounter many different emotions in its pages, there is humour as well; to get through something like this, you need humour, and a positive approach.

I am not a professional in any way, this is simply an account of my journey. All the information is intended for general knowledge and is not intended as a substitute for medical advice or treatment for brain tumours, or any other medical treatment. This information should not be used in place of a visit, call, consultation or advice of your doctor.

This book is dedicated to my parents, husband and son, who have been there every step of the way and have been so supportive and encouraging, and to my friends. Without their support (and chauffeuring services) I would have gone crazy.

Introduction

I was born on the 11th October 1975 in Casteau, Belgium, to Jean June Florence Short (formally Tenwick) and Robert Short and had an older sister, Melisa. Both my parents had been in the British Army, which was why I was born abroad. My mother came out of the Army more or less as soon as they were married.

My early years were spent travelling around the world with the Army. I guess a lot people would say I was lucky, but I was too young to remember most of it. We moved to England from Nepal, where I remember a few things - meeting some Gurkhas at the top of a very large hill, scorpions in the swimming pool (probably why I was such a fast swimmer) and hailstones the size of tennis balls in the monsoon season. One of the first memories I had of England was being told off for playing in the school sandpit – well, why have a sandpit if you can't play with it?

My father remained in London for two years on his own to complete his 22 years' service and commuted at weekends to Lincoln, where my parents were to make our home. When my father was invited to 'have lunch' with Her Majesty at Mill Hill barracks we were all invited to join him to celebrate his leaving, which made me very proud. He then joined the prison service. My mother worked too, doing a couple of part-time retail jobs. They didn't have it easy at first as this was the time when mortgages were around 14%.

I had what I would consider to be a normal upbringing; I was given everything I needed and never went without (unless you count the time my sister was given a ghetto blaster, and I looked at it longingly as I had been given a sewing machine!

I joined the Brownies, Guides, St John Ambulance and Air Cadets and swam a lot, even for my county. I learned ballet and tap dancing and was very active. My school life was relatively normal, although I did not settle well in my infant school in Mill Hill. It was my first experience at a proper school and I don't think I understood the rules properly. I laughed at what the teacher said, thinking it was funny. I played in the sandpit when I wasn't supposed to and I refused to leave my sister when she had a bad cut on her leg. It was time for a new school, though moving 150 miles north seemed a little extreme!

My parents described me as 'wild' and 'spirited' but I never had any behaviour problems at other schools. My first school in Lincoln I remember very well. I settled so well that I was moved up a year ahead of my time, although I was kept down the following year so that didn't work out!

I left school after GCSEs and managed to go straight into a job. I was only the office junior, but I felt very important going to work. On my first day I remember thinking it would also be my last, as I spilt a cup of coffee over the Managing Director's desk, all over his papers. Thankfully he just waved me out, so I made myself scarce.

I worked my way up in the company and then met my first husband. We were married for three years before having our son Lewis. During this time I studied for further qualifications, as I was beginning to regret not having an array of certificates. Unfortunately the marriage didn't work out for very long, but if we hadn't got together I would never have had Lewis (he is now 14).

I met my second husband, Roy, when I was working in Birmingham. To cut a very long story very short, after studying at University College Worcester we moved back to Lincoln, where I worked as a business support manager for the local authority. I loved the job, although they gave me a lot of grief and expected me to work miracles.

During this time my parents had decided to retire and move to Spain. I know a lot of Brits did this, but Mum and Dad had a house in a rural location and it was simply stunning. They continue working hard in the garden, so they are looking after my inheritance!

Roy and I were fortunate enough to travel a fair bit, particularly to the Caribbean, at least twice a year. I was spoilt by being able to buy Gucci shoes and handbags whenever I saw nice ones and would constantly get teased about wearing them to work at a local authority. My view was there is no point having them if you don't wear them. I had hair extensions, had my nails done – all by mobile beauticians, to cut the cost a bit, and it is more convenient if they come to you.

We had a busy social life. If we weren't travelling people would come and stay with us and we would be out partying and drinking. I would be running all over the place getting Lewis to school, football training, football games, going out for dinner - we lived our lives at a hundred miles per hour.

Who would have imagined the change that was about to come?

CHAPTER 1

Something's not right...

In October 2008 my life was delivered a cruel blow. Everybody knows their own body, and something wasn't right with mine. There was a definite tingle in my hand, which went away only when the hand was warm. My colleagues must have through I was mad or had an incontinence problem, as I kept going to the toilet and washing the hand with hot water. Finally the tingle disappeared from my hand, but not from my mind.

I have always been a worrier, and now that we have the internet, it was lethal. I typed in 'tingle in the hand' and diagnosed myself as having multiple sclerosis. I was gutted. What could be worse than MS?

I broke the news of my fears to my husband, Roy, when we were walking the dogs that evening. I broke down, in a field of all places. His response was quite rightly that I was being ridiculous, but I summoned the courage to make an appointment with my GP a few weeks later.

CHAPTER ONE

I was expecting to be told that I was being silly and to go away and not give it another thought. The response I got was quite different and did nothing to allay my fears.

'Nobody knows what's round the corner, just go with life and face things as we have to' said the doctor. That made me worry all the more. I wasn't happy with this and as we had private health insurance I asked to be referred to a neurologist – better safe than sorry.

My referral came through pretty quickly and I asked Roy to come with me to my appointment, which was at the private hospital in Lincoln with a very experienced neurologist.

I felt a bit foolish in front of this complete stranger telling him I thought I had a terrible disease. Talk about being a hypochondriac, but I knew I needed an answer or I would never get it out of my head, and something was still telling me things were not right.

I then found myself doing all sorts of strange activities in front of this man, including walking in a straight line with my eyes closed and touching my nose – I felt very foolish. As any sensible person would have expected, I was told there was no evidence of my having MS and I was a 'very healthy young lady'. But I still wasn't satisfied.

Given that I had private health insurance, the

neurologist agreed to perform an MRI scan and a nerve conduction test, both of which he expected to come back negative. There was a sense of annoyance from my husband as he considered it unnecessary, but he knew I would not take the word from anyone unless there was evidence – these tests were evidence, and he asked that they should be done.

The date for my scan came through for the end of October 2008 and the nerve function test in the first week of November. I was sure they would provide the evidence I needed to calm myself down and get on with life.

Having never had an MRI before I was unsure what to expect. I was extremely glad of ear defenders - what a noise! I was asked to lie down on what can only be described as a shelf. A mask was then put over my head and fixed so that I did not move my head during the scan.

Then came the noise. It was like thunder rumbling at first, then it sounded as if I had my head in a tin can and someone was hitting it with a hammer. That was bad enough, and then the machine started vibrating. When I opened my eyes I felt somewhat claustrophic, so I closed them quickly.

The whole scan probably lasted about 30 minutes, but it felt longer. I couldn't wait to get out. With that over I started to relax and look forward to getting the results back – yes actually look forward to them, so that I could get on with life.

But when I heard the answering machine message the next day I had a terribel feeling. It was asking me to go for another scan with 'contrast' to show more clearly what they had seen. This wasn't the reassuring result I had wanted!

It was Friday. How on earth what I going to get a result by the weekend? But the team at the hospital was fantastic and I could have asked no more. The consultant neurologist agreed to come in on the Saturday morning to read the scans and tell us what they meant. What a difference private health care makes!

CHAPTER 2

Diagnosis

We agreed to meet the neurologist on Saturday morning at the private hospital, and it was there that I was told I had a tumour. A brain tumour.

I couldn't believe what I was hearing. Oh my God, this was serious. Typical me, always unique.

My first thought was that this was better than MS, as it was operable - wasn't it? The neurologist actually told us it wasn't serious, but he couldn't look me in the eye. I had liked him before I came into the room.

I took some time off work, as I had to get my head round this (excuse the pun) and meet a whole new group of people who would now play a big part in my life and offer me support all the way along. It didn't help though. How would I tell my parents? How would I tell my son, Lewis? He was only 10.

I was given an appointment with a consultant neurosurgeon (it was still sinking in that I actually had to meet a brain surgeon) and my husband and I went to see him three days later.

CHAPTER TWO

It was a great relief to hear that the tumour was benign. It was a World Health Organisation (WHO) grade 2 astrocytoma, and I had probably had it some time.

The choices discussed during the multi-disciplinary team (MDT) meeting were 1) remove it (I wasn't really up for that one) 2) perform a biopsy, which still meant drilling a hole in my head or 3) leave it alone and keep an eye on it. This seemed mad! But this was the surgeon's preferred option as it was not showing any signs of growth (they call it 'watch and wait') and it was felt best to leave it well alone – you have to trust your medical team.

I found myself telling people it was OK, when really I was terrified. This 'thing' inside my brain could start growing at any time. My world had just entered a new phase of being that was to be my new 'normal', as it was to be my new way of life. It was to involve regular MRI scans, Macmillan nurses, neurologists, neurosurgeons, radiographers and hospital appointments.

Dealing with my emotions during this time was tough. I was just beginning to get used to it when my next MRI scan was due. During the first 12 months they wanted to scan me at three months, then three months later, then six months, so they could get a timeline. If it had not showed any signs of growing I would be moved to six-monthly scans.

I was incredibly scared this time because I knew it was in there and had been trying to protect it to make sure it didn't grow. I had to try and get on with a 'normal' life. I decided, as the tumour was part of me, to name it, and so Tallulah was created, a fitting name for something so rare.

Types of brain tumour

I researched brain tumours and found there to be many different types as follows:

Gliomas: Most tumours develop from the supporting cells in the brain, known as glial cells. More than half of brain tumours are gliomas. These can be:

Astrocytomas, made up of star-shaped cells called astrocytes. These can be slow growing (grade 1 or 2) or fast growing (grade 3 or 4) (Grade 3 is often referred to as an anaplastic astrocytoma). Grade 4 is very fast growing and is referred to as glioblastoma multiforme (GBM). Grades 1 and 2 can often be completely removed with surgery, whereas 3 and 4 are more difficult and are often followed up with radiotherapy and chemotherapy.

Ependymomas are a rare form of glioma and develop from ependymal cells. They are graded 1 to 3 and respond well to surgery but can spread to other parts of the brain and spinal cord.

Oligodendrogliomas are formed with oligodendrocytes and can be grade 2 or high grade. These tumours have a tendency to grow into the surrounding brain tissue so generally cannot be removed in their entirety and can grow so slowly after being removed that you may be well for a long time after. Once again radiotherapy and chemotherapy are used to treat the higher grade ones.

Meningiomas form in the meninges (covering the brain). About 25% of brain tumours fall into this category. They are graded 1, 2 and 3, 1 being the lowest grade. They are mainly slow growing and it is usually possible to remove them – depending where they are in the brain. It is preferred for individuals to undergo radiotherapy for grade 2 and 3 tumours

Primitive neuroectodermal tumour (PNET): Medulloblastoma is the most common type of this tumour. More than half are diagnosed in children and attempts are made to remove them completely by surgery.

Pituitary: These are always benign. The small non-hormone-producing ones do not usually come back after surgery but the larger hormone producing ones are more difficult to control. The difficulty is in controlling the hormones that the tumours produce.

Haemangioblastoma tumours are rare and develop from the cells that line the blood vessels. These are generally very slow growing and depending on their location in the brain, can be removed by surgery.

Acoustic neoromas develop in the acoustic or auditory nerve. These are usually benign tumours nearly always curable by surgery, possibly with the introduction of radiotherapy.

Pineal region tumours develop in the pineal gland. These are rare and radiotherapy is the treatment of choice here.

Spinal cord tumours: These tumours can grow both inside and outside the spinal cord and treatment varies as to the location. They are usually treated by surgery followed by radiotherapy.

Primary central nervous system lymphomas are malignant tumours of the lymphatic system. This is a rare condition and is difficult to treat. Chemotherapy and radiotherapy is the preferred treatment but depending on age and health whole brain radiation may be the best option.

According to Cancer Research UK: 'Overall for all types of malignant brain tumours in adults, more than a third of people diagnosed (36%) live for at least a year. About 15 out of every 100 people diagnosed (15%) live for more than 5 years after diagnosis. Just under 10 out of every 100 people diagnosed (10%) live for more than 10 years after diagnosis. Women seem to do slightly better than men, but we don't know why this is.'

I was diagnosed as having an astrocytoma.

* Macmillan last reviewed this information in 2009 and Cancer Research UK reviewed it in 2012

CHAPTER 3

October 2009 - wakey wakey!

After a very stressful time at work I was greatly looking forward to ten days in St Lucia. My parents came over from Spain, where they had lived for the past seven years or so, to look after the little chap and we headed off.

We were fortunate enough to be flying upper class with Virgin, and I found it very strange that I fell asleep in my seat before we had taken off. I never usually sleep on planes unless I am lying down.

On the second day there we met some Canadian friends of ours, and it was then that I experienced my first partial seizure. My arm was twitching uncontrollably and I had a strong urge to throw a bottle around the room. It was terrifying. I searched the internet for explanations, but deep down I knew something was very wrong.

I had several more experiences during the holiday, and my husband kept trying to dismiss them as anything but the explanation we feared. Even my

Macmillan nurse tried to reassure me that it could be just a virus, but I know my body and this was no virus.

When we returned home the twitches continued. Then they reduced and eventually they disappeared. My dad couldn't understand why it was always my right hand, so I had to explain that the tumour was sitting within the brain mechanisms that controlled my right hand, so something clearly was wrong. Unfortunately my parents had to return to Spain, and we decided that as things had settled we would just wait for the scan. It was due in January, so there wasn't too long to wait. Then we would just have to clear the 'good news if you don't hear within 48 hours' period and settle back down to normal life.

CHAPTER 4

January 2010 – MRI Scan

After a week we had heard nothing, so we celebrated with champagne, as did my parents and friends. Maybe I had to put my faith in the medical team after all. Or maybe not.

I was sitting in a meeting when I received an answering machine message asking me to call my neurosurgeon's secretary. He wanted to talk to me about my scan, which had been arranged for a week's time. A whole week - I don't think so! Fortunately my husband moved it forward to three days away, but even so those three days felt like three months.

I guess deep down I had expected it. The dreams I had always had about the tumour disappearing were clearly just that - dreams.

On the day of the scan I sat in the waiting room to be called through. When we were in there I noticed that there was a nursing assistant in the room, although there had never been anyone present before.

The words came out: 'The January scan showed something was changing.' What? The nursing assistant described it as 'an egg in which the yolk is going bad'. I'd always hated eggs. Now I hated them even more.

I was once again given three options: 1) leave it and scan again in three months, 2) a biopsy to see what was happening or 3) remove as much as they could (which I was told was around 90% or possibly all of it). This is known as debulking and resecting. The choice was obvious really. I'd wanted it removed as soon as I knew it was there anyway.

Plans were made there and then for me to go to Sheffield in two days' time to have a functional MRI, which would protect as much of my right side as possible, particularly my right hand. I had managed quite well in the consulting room to hold it together but broke down in the hallway – brain surgery, oh God, why couldn't it be something simple? My parents, how would I tell them? My son, how would I tell him? The nightmare was just beginning.

My husband phoned my parents and broke the awful news. They wanted to fly over immediately, but we were able to persuade them to wait until I was due back home, when I would need their help. My sister didn't seem to understand the seriousness of it as she felt it was all precautionary, but they don't open your head and mess with your brain unless they have to.

CHAPTER FOUR

Then I had to decide how to break the news to my son. He was due on a school trip to France, so I decided not to tell him until later. I wanted him to have a fantastic trip. It would all be over and done with and I would be home for when he got back – I was sure he'd forgive me and understand why I did it.

That week was very hard, trying to behave normally around him when I was breaking inside. I drove everywhere that week, as I knew I was going to have to surrender my driving licence for six months, devastating news as that was my independence done – how would I manage? How would I get my son to and from school (there was no bus)? I knew these things were a secondary priority, but they still bothered me.

Reality set in when my son went to his father's parents for the weekend and the dogs went to the kennels. The house was so quiet. I decided to use the silence to write letters to my husband and son – just in case something went wrong and I didn't come through the operation, I still wanted to have the final word! I knew I had to speak to my son before he left on the Monday to tell him I loved him, or I'd never settle.

Why was this happening to me? I wasn't a bad person, I'd been a good child, I believed I was a good mother and wife, I had never smoked or drunk much, so why me? I gathered it was going to be my new 'normal' to feel like this...

CHAPTER 5

February 2010 - the operation

My operation was scheduled for last on the list on Tuesday 16th February, but I had to have bloods, observations etc all done the day before and my surgeon had to set up the computer, so I had to have another MRI scan. However we managed to persuade him and the nursing staff to allow me to have all that done on the 15th February, but stay in the hotel round the corner with my husband that night.

We met with the surgeon and anaesthetist before we left and I joked with them that I had had my hair done, so I didn't want too much hair taken off, and that I had shaved my legs and arms so I'd made an effort. I said it to break the ice really! It was very strange to be eating lobster and drinking champagne with a medical bracelet on (the anaesthetist said I could have a small glass) but it kept my spirits up and distracted me from the seriousness of the situation. I even said the tumour could stay where it was, but we both knew that this was not an option. Tomorrow I would be fighting for my life.

I actually slept rather well that night. My worst trauma was having to hand my iPhone over for my husband to take care of. I felt I had lost the use of my hand already.

The wait was awful. Then I had to have a 'sat nav' attached to my head and little areas had to be shaved – oh lord, if the surgeon needed sat nav to tell him where the front and back were, was he the right surgeon?

I was scheduled for around 5 pm, so I started getting nervous once they told me to get into my theatre gown and put my surgical stockings on. It was really happening, they were actually going to play with my brain. Or as my surgeon had said months earlier 'amuse myself debulking your tumour'.

I tried hard to keep the tears back as I left the ward, but they still flowed. I told my anaesthetist, who had been laughing and joking with me the previous day, to make sure I didn't wake up in surgery. That was it. It all went dark, and I was in their hands.

I remember my surgeon asking me to wriggle the fingers on my right hand – they all moved, thankfully, then it went dark again.

The next thing I remembered was coming out of a

lift and hearing my husband's voice. There was no mistaking his accent. No matter what he says he's still a 'brummie'!

He came with me but was told to hold back until I was sorted on the ward. Still it must have been reassuring for him, as the fear in his voice was unbearable when I got out of the lift – he really did care!

It wasn't until I saw the photo of me straight from surgery that I realized how poorly I looked. I had wires attached all over me and an oxygen mask on my face, very fetching. I was really sleepy but was able to have my husband sitting with me for a few minutes before I fell asleep.

I awoke a couple of hours later really needing the toilet and was quite surprised when the nursing staff asked if I had been out of bed yet. I had just had brain surgery and had only been on the ward for two hours, don't they read the patients' notes? I wasn't allowed out of bed and had to get myself on to a bedpan, how embarrassing, they are god-awful things and I had so much sympathy now for all the patients I had had to help on to them. 'Please don't tip' was all I could think.

So, I'd done it, I'd survived, it was over. Time to recover now and get back on my feet – five months and twenty nine days to go until I get my driving licence back...

CHAPTER FIVE

Ouch, I had a headache. I had expected one, but not like this. They gave me pain medication, but I had a feeling it was the medication that was making me feel bad. It was codeine, phosphate and paracetamol – excuse me, I've just had brain surgery, where's the morphine? Apparently they don't like patients to have morphine as they can't keep an eye on your vital signs when you're on it.

I have to say, most of the staff who took care of me were useless. Considering I had gone 'private' I expected a better standard of care. They might have thought I was sleeping at night, but most of the time I wasn't and I was observing everything, the staff nattering to each other, talking about the very poorly patients. It was sad really, and I wanted to get out of there quickly. The only way that was going to happen was if I could get well fast.

The next morning I managed to give myself a bed bath and put pyjamas on. I wasn't quite ready for clubbing yet, but I was on my way. Visiting times were daft, 3 pm till 4, then 6 till 7. I felt sorry for both my husband and myself, we were both bored. I couldn't understand why, as I was a private patient, they weren't more relaxed. I understood why I had been in intensive care initially, but why I had to wait two nights to get a private room was beyond me.

Thankfully I only had to spend three nights in there before being allowed home – scary really. To get home I had to show that I could manage stairs – I practically ran up them, much to the amusement of the nurses. Then I had to pass a mini mental test which consisted of questions. I was given a road name and told I needed to remember it as it would be asked again at the end of the test – I failed! I knew I would never remember the answer to that question, as I have never been good with road names.

So the good news was, I was being allowed home. Fantastic - life was going to get back to normal. My surgeon told me he would come and have a chat with me before I left and I put my gorgeous new Juicy Couture tracksuit on, which my husband had bought me especially to go home in. Having had my turban removed and replaced with what can only be described as a big plaster really doing nothing at all, I looked beautiful! They had done an amazing job and I had barely lost any hair at all. My husband came early and we were just waiting for me to be discharged.

Then it came, out of nowhere, a huge blow. My surgeon broke the news that my tumour had been promoted – it had gone up a grade. It was now a Grade 3 (even though it was only just changing from Grade 2, it was still classed as a 3). That was bad enough in itself, but this news meant that I would not be allowed to drive for two years. The final blow was that I would need a course of six weeks of daily radiotherapy, just in case there were any cells left, and 'to give me a better chance in the future'.

In a few minutes I had gone from a cheery girl who was going home to a tear-stained girl who was devastated. It felt like a death sentence all over again, though at least my surgeon had made it clear that there had been absolutely no signs of it becoming a Grade 4 (though he had admitted he was worried) and that a Grade 3 was much easier to treat than a Grade 4.

No wonder he hadn't been able to look me in the eye. Just two days earlier he had told me the scans looked good and showed no signs of the tumour, and he was now saying that they had 'maybe' left some behind. Brilliant.

I just wanted to get home. I don't know how I did it, but we stopped off at Starbucks before facing my parents.

Fortunately for me my husband had already broken the news to them, so all that awaited me was a great big hug.

CHAPTER 6

March 2010 - radiotherapy

For radiotherapy they have to make a mask, so they take a mould of your head, which is quite scary as there is only a small hole to breathe out of, but it only takes a few minutes. It was at this point that I mentioned hair loss. My surgeon said, and I quote: 'You will lose some hair but it will grow back within twelve months'. I asked the nursing assistant whether I would get away with a wide parting, as there was a line on the mask and I thought the hair loss would follow this line. She replied that I might, as I was only having two 'zap zones'. Not true, as it turned out.

I went back to the hospital a few days later for a 'dry run' and to test the mask. I sat down on the bed and asked the staff to show me on the mask where the zap zones were. I burst into tears. It was the whole left side of my head and some of the middle. Not only that but I would get exit radiotherapy damage on the right and at the back of my head.

CHAPTER SIX

I kept hoping that it wouldn't be as bad as all that, but I had my hair cut about four inches in preparation and to make the mask more comfortable. My first radiotherapy session was just a few days away. This tumour was going to be blasted into orbit!

I can tell anyone undergoing radiotherapy who is given hope that they might not lose their hair - it is most definitely a myth. My blasts were fine for the first seven or so, and then I started to notice that my hair was coming out everywhere. It was heartbreaking, as I adored my hair. I had stupidly thought that it only happened with chemotherapy. Nobody I had known had lost their hair with radiotherapy.

I ended up pulling out long strands and handfuls and dropping them on the floor, as I couldn't bear to look at it. My husband picked them up. At this point I wished that the staff had been more honest as I would have had all my hair cut off, but it was too late. My head was now too sore from the radiotherapy burns to be shaved.

My husband was helping me with the cream they provided, but instead of being careful with the application he was being very generous and I ended up having to wash it all off. I didn't get any more pain from burns though!

By the time my radiotherapy had finished I only had

a 1 mm strip of hair where my fringe used to be and a perfect circle of hair at the back of my head. Everything else had gone. Nobody could understand how unfeminine this made me feel. I couldn't bear to look at myself, which was incredibly difficult as I walk past mirrors every morning, when I clean my teeth.

I cried regularly, usually when I was in bed on my own. My son was so good about it all and it never bothered him. He just kept telling me 'it'll grow back mum'. Bless him, but that didn't make me feel better.

Feb 2010 - My meal
before my op

Feb 2010 - Getting ready
for the 'sat nav'

The 'sat nav'

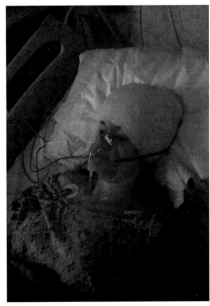

Feb 2010 - ICU

Feb 2010 - The morning after

Feb 2010 - Leaving hospital
4 days after

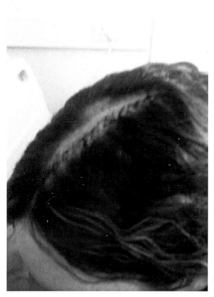

Feb 2010 - My war wound

Feb 2010 - Starbucks on
way home

April 10 - Radiotherapy mask

July 2010 - Roy's 50th birthday

July 2010 - Roy 50th Roy and I

July 2010 - Family holiday in
Tenerife, Roy's actual birthday

July 2010 - Me with my mum, dad and Lewis in Tenerife

Sept 10 - Chemo Card made for
me by a friend

Sept 10 - My pre-chemotherapy
party bottle bin

Christmas 2010
still trying to enjoy it

Christmas 2010

Dec 2010 - Chistmas I found it
too tiring

Dec 2010 - Christmas
me and dad

Dec 2010- Lewis with the
Christmas sausage rolls

Dec 2010 - New Year's Eve

Aug 2012 - Belgium Grand Prix
off chemotherapy

Sept 2012 - MacMillan
cake baking

Nov 2011 - London Ice Bar

Dec 2011 - A better Christmas

Dec 2011 - New year, new start

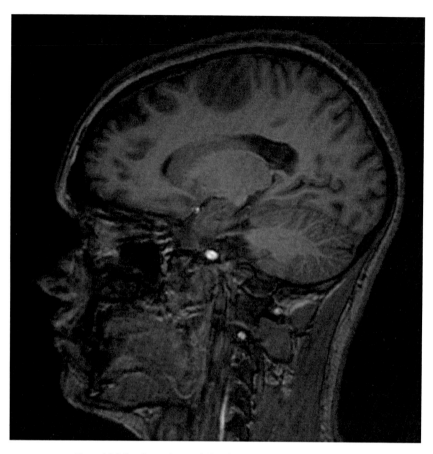

Oct 1998 - Incidental finding - tumour sleeping

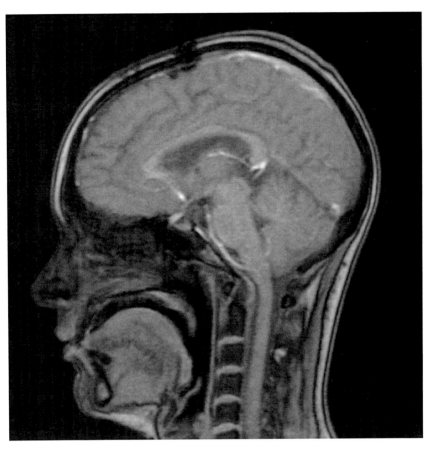

Feb 2010 - Post op photo - no sign of tumour

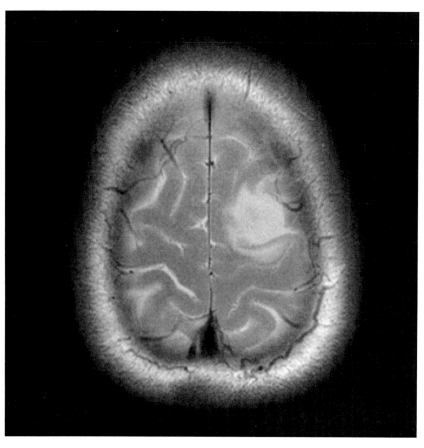

August 2010 - Post-radiotherapy - tumour back to same size

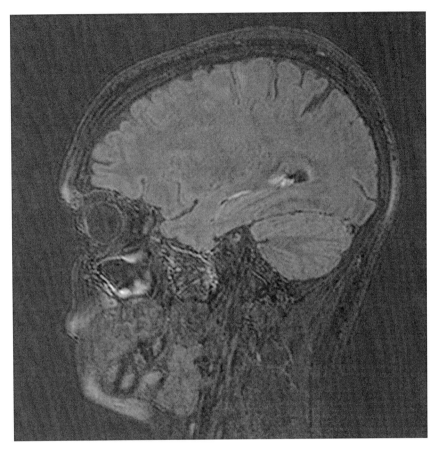

Jan 2012 - Post-chemotherapy - no sign of tumour

CHAPTER 7

July 22nd 2010 - Roy's 50th birthday party

Before my illness I had been making preparations for my husband's 50th birthday celebrations. I was organizing a casino night and had booked a function room at our local pub. It was meant to be a surprise, but I now told him I was organizing it as keeping it a secret would not be possible now.

When he told me he didn't really want a party I knew that he was just trying to take the pressure off me – I knew that if anybody liked partying it was him! To be honest, it was a welcome distraction. Although it was no longer a surprise, I did manage to hire a stretched limo for the family without him knowing, which was a result, along with an Aston Martin lookalike cake and a picture collage of all the children, so he didn't know everything!

Everyone had a fantastic night, all getting dressed up and partying the night away. It showed me that life does go on, and you can still have a life and celebrate.

My energy levels had dropped severely. I was so tired, but I didn't want to give in to it. My mum was brilliant, cooking lots of pasta and vegetables, but I was still very tired. Deep down I was dreading having to cope with the two-week family holiday we had booked for my husband's birthday, but again I was determined to continue life as normal.

I remember one point when I was trying bikinis on to go on a family holiday and I broke down, saying how ugly I looked. I never tried anything on again after that without wearing a wig.

On holiday I hated the fact that I couldn't lie in the sun, that it was difficult to go in the pool, that I had to try and have a sleep in the afternoon, and I couldn't drink cocktails round the pool. It was so much effort to get ready to go out in the evenings, and then I had to go back to the room early after dinner as I was worn out. At least I didn't have to cook though, and as it was 'all inclusive' there was always something I fancied to eat – not that I had been cooking, with my mum being over.

We managed to celebrate my husband's actual birthday and a few members of our party had a few too many… big mistake, as it was my son's birthday the next day. Another reason to celebrate, he was officially a teenager, arrghh!

I was still so tired when we got back. Then I found

out why – I had somnolence syndrome, which means the brain is shutting down and rebooting itself. Apparently a lot of young women get it, especially mothers – why hadn't anybody warned me and told me I was normal?

A break at my mum and dad's house in Spain was far more relaxing. I was trying hard to get off my steroids but kept having headaches, so I gave up. I thought I would deal with that when I got home. I had emailed my Macmillan nurse, so she knew I had not been able to get off them and she agreed to let me take them until I got home.

It was when I was at my parent's house that I did the unthinkable and googled 'survival times' for brain tumours. Big mistake – never go there, the information is inaccurate and out of date and every individual is different (I learned this later on from my support group site). I had frightened myself so much, but could not tell anyone as they would just tell me to stay off the computer. I wanted to go home, I wanted my scan, I wanted good news, and I wanted it to be over.

CHAPTER 8

28th August 2010 - Tallulah comes back

A lesson to learn - believe your body and listen to it. If something feels wrong, push it with the medical teams!

My headaches were trying to tell me that Tallulah was back, just as she had been before. I travelled to Sheffield to review the results of my scan with my surgeon, as the Macmillan nurse I was supported by at the time had told us it was not operable.

I was devastated to learn that the tumour was almost back to the size it had been before surgery and radiotherapy. So much for 'I think I got it all, but want you to have radiotherapy as a precaution'. It seemed I had lost my hair and endured radiotherapy for nothing. But on the positive side, my surgeon said that in fact it was operable.

My first thought was to get it out, to operate again. Apparently they had a rather heated discussion about my situation at the MDT (Multi-Disciplinary Team) meeting as to what treatment to carry out and it was their opinion that chemotherapy should be the next step. The nurse who had telephoned to break the news to me had indicated that the tumour was inoperable, but that was not the case. My surgeon did not want to operate again as the next step just in case he left a seed behind, and I would need chemotherapy anyway – which would have to be delayed to allow my wound to heal. I had to trust my medical team and hope they were right.

My surgeon agreed to speak to the oncology team in Lincoln as a matter of urgency – he actually telephoned when we were there and left a message. Again I found myself having to tell family and friends the dreadful news. When will it ever be good news?

Naturally everyone was disappointed, but we all had to remain positive and strong. I was honest with my son, who I have to say took it very well. I was going to have to have chemo to blast this invader, but was reassured that there were some chemotherapy drugs that were very nasty and this wasn't one of them.

Before the chemotherapy began I decided to have a party. Well – any excuse! I wasn't sure how many people would come as I had found that a lot of people around us simply did not know how to handle it.

However, we had more than a houseful! Thank goodness it was a warm, dry day and we were able to spill outside.

I took advantage of being able to drink alcohol, as I knew that I wouldn't be able to drink again for some time. We had all the other things I wouldn't be able to have, including cheese. It was a fantastic party, especially as it had been organized very much at the last minute.

I chuckled as I was given a pre-chemo card, which was handmade so it was all the more special. The party went on into the night and I had to apologise to the dustmen when they collected the bin, as it was heaving with bottles. There were a few sore heads the next day, though fortunately for a change not mine!

I decided after that night that I would have to celebrate my end of chemo too, when it came.

Sickness was all I could think of. I'd already lost my hair for nothing, so I wasn't frightened of that. I'd been warned that there are always delays when going to 'that room' (we nicknamed it that as people went in and never came out) for treatment, and now I was going there. I felt sick and needed the toilet many times during my treatment. Today was no different. Fortunately there wasn't too much of a delay and I had to just tell myself 'onwards and upwards'. Tallulah, you are causing me a lot of trouble!

I was to have six cycles of PCV chemotherapy (Procarbazine, Lomustine (CCNU) and Vincristine). My regimen (schedule) was to be ten days on chemo and 32 days off until I had completed all six cycles, plus various blood tests along the way to check it was standing up to the drugs. The Vincristine was intravenously infused, the others were in tablet form, which I was able to take home, along with anti-sickness tablets – it all sounded straightforward.

CHAPTER 9

September 2010 -
first chemotherapy cycle

My first cycle was set for September 23. On the day the nurse explained various dos and don'ts, what not to eat and what to look out for. Within an hour and a half my first introduction was over and I had had my first dose of poison.

Again I questioned what I had done to deserve this, why doesn't it happen to criminals? I soon learned that cancer makes no distinction about who it chooses; rich or poor, young or old, good citizens or 'scum'.

I took some comfort from the singer Russell Watson. Surely if he could beat a giant tumour, I could beat mine. I even prayed before I took my tablets that night – I was religious about taking my anti-sickness tablet, then an hour later the rest of the poison concoction and off to sleep, here we go...

I have to say that other than a bit of nausea the chemo went rather well. I even managed a shopping trip with a close friend, and boy can she shop! We managed to fill the back of the car, and it was a very big car!

It was the first time in a long time that I had actually forgotten I was poorly. I noticed that I got tired more quickly and had to take several coffee breaks, but the ten days soon passed. If this is what chemotherapy is like, I should be able to get on with daily living.

One question we had asked the chemotherapy nurses before I started the course was whether your first cycle was an indication as to how your body was going to react to them all, and we were told it was. Another question we asked was whether you could take build-up drinks. We were told not as they may interfere with the chemo. I'm not sure either of those answers were right.

Other than watching the foods you couldn't eat and avoiding people with colds and viruses, I carried on as normal, and before I knew it it the cycle was done with.

CHAPTER 10

November 2010 – second cycle

I wasn't worried when I went for my second cycle on November 4 as I felt I knew what to expect. I also had the bonus of Mum and Dad being with me – I was thankful that they were able to come over again from Spain. My dad took on the role of chauffeur and my mum did a great deal; washing, ironing, cooking, fattening up the dog!

Mum came into 'The Room' for my second lot of treatment so that she could fully understand it all. I remember her saying to me that she never thought she'd be going through chemotherapy with one of her children. I had to wipe a tear away before she saw it.

The treatment was a little more painful this time. Once they had the IV in and the Vincristine started flowing it stung a bit. It didn't last long but it was painful all the same.

Once it had finished I took my bags of pills and went home. This time I decided to take my anti-sickness tablets as soon as we got home rather than at 9 pm. I look the rest of my cocktail at 10 pm when I went to bed as I had done previously, and went to sleep.

Taking the tablets on arrival home proved to be a big mistake. I awoke in the early hours and was terribly sick for quite a while. The tablets had obviously worn off before the poison had cleared my system, but thankfully I had kept it down long enough so as not to have to go and have it all again. I wouldn't make that mistake again!

Over the next few days I felt completely drained. I had acid reflux and an incredibly sore throat. An aversion to toilet fresheners which I had developed during pregnancy was back. I took Merocaine for the sore throat and was prescribed Omeprazole for the acid. The tablets I had to take were growing in number.

My appetite had reduced, but I was still eating. I just had to eat what I fancied, but a lot of the time it was only nibbling. I think the thing I found the hardest was drinking water – who drinks water? I couldn't really stand tea or coffee (I had been pretty much addicted to them before). I tried milk, but that sat too heavy in my stomach.

This was when having my parents was so beneficial for me. They made sure I ate and drank. Dad made me a cup of very weak tea as soon as I got up, then he used a rather noisy coffee machine to make frothy coffee, again weak but better than instant. It had milk in it so it was doing me good, and fingers crossed it was giving me some energy. Dad then made some form of breakfast – there was no skipping it. If I had been on my own I probably wouldn't have bothered.

Mum had the tricky task of cooking something I'd be likely to fancy. It's important that people around you encourage you and congratulate you on what you've eaten, rather than keep trying to make you eat more. However, water is definitely your friend during chemotherapy, it flushes the poison out – I used to be able to smell the chemo on my body, on my clothes and my bedding, I hated it. It also keeps your body hydrated – I struggled a little with constipation this cycle round and I put that down to not drinking enough water. I was so glad to have finished my second cycle. But the next cycle, my third, would be bang on Christmas. Great!

CHAPTER 11

December 2010 - third cycle

I had learned my lesson for my third cycle on December 16 and took the anti-sickness tablet an hour before my others. I wasn't actually sick this time – I just felt incredibly nauseous. My big problem this time round was constipation. I had terrible stomach cramps and the only way I could get relief was to either have a hot water bottle on both my lower back and stomach or lay in the foetal position. Although this eased it, I knew I had to walk to try to get things moving, and I found Cura-Heat and ThermCare heatwraps brilliant.

I had been prescribed so many laxatives; surely one of them would work? It's quite amusing looking back. Every time I went to the bathroom I was greeted by people asking if I had 'been'!

Countless times I went to and from the doctors getting more and more medication, each stronger than the last. I'm sure it was the threat of being admitted to hospital on Christmas Eve that finally sorted me out for my third cycle, though the doctor would say it was the Movicol – awful stuff but it was my friend this time round. Could you imagine being admitted on Christmas Eve? I'd never have been out in time for Christmas.

CHAPTER 12

Christmas 2010

We'd all been looking forward to Christmas. Deep down I had a fear that it would be my last, so I wanted to make sure my family had a really good one. It also helped me take my mind off things. I wanted this Christmas to be special, but in the event I was too poorly and we had to open our presents in stages. I fell asleep on the settee with my Santa hat on and listened to all those around me saying what a shame it was.

I just wept quietly to myself - damn tumour! I felt I had spoiled Christmas. Dinner looked lovely, but I really couldn't eat it. I had no appetite at all and just wanted to be in bed, on my own. I couldn't even have a glass of champagne, but the sausage rolls didn't get away, I managed a couple of them. No cheese biscuits though, blast this no-cheese rubbish.

I was so happy to have taken my last chemo tablet on Boxing Day – that was it, I was half way through.

Even better, we had a second Christmas dinner the day after Boxing Day and I thoroughly enjoyed it this time. I ate really well, for me – lots of vegetables!

My energy levels were still sluggish and I have to say I don't know how I'd have managed without help. Was this normal? I guess so. So much for the way your body copes. Question is, how would I cope, all the way through?

I managed to celebrate New Year with everyone, feeling quite well – I even remembered to pop my gravy granules in my handbag (the ones used by restaurants always seemed to contain yeast extract, which I was not allowed to have) and sneak a sip of champagne. I finally started to feel more positive about my future, although the first scan was looming and I already had that on my mind.

CHAPTER 13

2011 – the last leg

I'm not a religious person, but thank you God for giving me good news at last. The tumour was stable and even showed slight shrinkage. All the terrible side effects were worth it, it was working. To have shrinkage was more than I could possibly have hoped for - yabba dabba doo!

Fourth cycle – January 27 2011

Bloods were OK, so let's get cracking. I had never drunk so much water in my life. Mum was putting vegetables in everything, which my son found hilarious – spaghetti bolognese with carrots and broccoli? I'm not sure which was worse, the constipation or the nausea – probably the constipation.

Off to the doctor to get something stronger than my last cycle – he had given up any form of examination now and just prescribed laxatives. He knew I was more than able to use them correctly myself, which to be fair, I was very happy about. So far I had had Lactalose, senna, Microlax enema, Bisacodyl suppository, Dulcolax and Movicol – quite a concoction.

I was getting concerned about my weight loss at this point. I was eating very little, which was not helping the constipation, but I was trying to drink water. People who visited commented on the weight loss. At this point I was a size 6, so my clothes started to hang off me. Online shopping was necessary; there was no way I could go round the shops. But the treatment was working, which did give me a psychological boost.

Peripheral neuropathy, as they call it, started to bother me a little on this cycle, and was worse when I had a bath, which I did every night. Quite a strange feeling - not quite pins and needles, more like an electrical impulse. The only think I could liken it to was a tense machine, the device they use to help women during labour, which they had used for me when I was pregnant. It affected my feet and my legs.

The hand where the IV was attached was also very sore this time round, to the point where nobody could touch it about two days after the infusion and I had to be careful where I put it at night. Again the bath made this worse, so I didn't put it in the bath (I did wash myself though, with the other hand!) This problem went away by itself, but even now when my hands get really cold and the veins stand out, they get tender.

Fifth cycle – 10th March – My sixth wedding anniversary

Here we go again, but I'm almost there. When we met with my consultant two days before my chemo started, I mentioned my concern about my weight loss and we were asked if I had been taking build-up drinks. I had never been told to take them - what a disgrace. I had lost almost three stone, and I had been just under nine before I started. Unbelievable. To make it worse, I was entitled to them free of charge!

I began taking them immediately. Banana and strawberry Complan tasted just like milk shakes and had all the vitamins and nutrients I needed in them. I wished I had been taking them from the start.

My arm was very sore this time, as the nurse who administered it was new to the job, great. So I prepared myself for it to be very sore in two days' time. At least now I knew it would get better in time.

I was very tired this time round despite all the carbohydrate meals I had been eating (well, trying to eat). Then my good old friend constipation hit. I added sodium picosulfate to this mix, but nothing. The cramps were worse than ever. At one point I wanted to give up. The pain was terrible.

I went to see the doctor, who prescribed me a morphine patch for the back pain and said I wasn't constipated – she said it would take 12 hours to work but then last for five days. I went home and took codeine to get me through the night (I know they can cause constipation too, but I was desperate).

I woke that night still in a lot of pain and we called the out-of-hours emergency response team, who were brilliant. They told me to stay at home away from bugs and they would come to me. Apparently the patch wasn't morphine, it was codeine, so I had overdosed on codeine.

They also gave me some different anti-sickness medication that was put behind your tongue so it didn't go through your digestive system – I have to say that when I started to use it it was not great. I was still in pain two days later. That was 10 days of not being able to go to the toilet, so I was admitted. I told the doctors all the medications I had tried and asked them to bring the big guns out, but they insisted on doing it their way. I ended up staying in for two days before they listened and used a big gun. It was a lemon powder drink and tasted like Lemsip, and boy it did the trick. No colonic irrigation required for me!

I was so glad to get home. Cycle five done!

Cycle six – April 21

My bloods weren't great this time around. I was due to have my final chemo session on the 21st April, but my red cell count was too low - it had to be 100 or above and mine was hovering around 90 - so I had to go away and try again the next week.

Mum was in her element adding vegetables to everything. Fortunately I wasn't allowed liver so she couldn't make me eat that! The next week the red cell count was even lower. What could I try that I hadn't already tried? I had already tried papaya and papaya juice – eugh! So I put my faith in acupuncture, which hurt like hell, but I was reassured that they do it to many patients and it does work. If my bloods weren't at 100 this time round, then they were going to call it a day. But I was determined to do all six cycles - surely that would give me the best possible chance?

On 17th May my red bloods were spot on 100, but even now that they were as required, my consultant gave me the choice as to whether I wanted cycle six, given how rough cycle five had been. Hell yeah! Who wouldn't?

The very next day I was in 'the room' receiving my infusion of deadly toxins for the last time. I must admit I wasn't looking forward to it after the last cycle, but it had to be done. I was strong, and had to believe in myself.

I started the lactulose immediately, then the water and the Movicol and even added short walks to try and keep things moving, but no, my old friend constipation joined me again. It was 10 days this time, which had to be a record. He was such a familiar visitor this time I even thought of giving him a name - Cyril!

When I visited my doctor he actually asked me what worked for me and said that if I hadn't been by the next day he would prescribe me 'the yellow drink', which apparently they are only meant to prescribe to end-of-life patients. Well let me tell you, when you haven't been in 10 days, with the cramps, pains and hard stomach and the pain you know you're going to get passing, you do feel like you are at the end of your life.

The relief! I certainly don't need a colonic irrigation this month either! I suffered chest pain the day afterwards and had an ambulance, a Lives vehicle and an ambulance car answer the call – the neighbours were bound to have been alerted with all the blue lights. After having an oxygen mask on for 15 minutes, they insisted that I go to hospital to get checked out because I was on chemotherapy, so I had my second ride in an ambulance – they really are comfortable you know!

CHAPTER THIRTEEN

I was discharged within an hour with the 'lemon drink' being marked down as the culprit.

That was it, all six cycles were done. Now I really could recover and my parents could go back to their home in Spain. I felt so sorry that they had had to leave it all that time, as I know how much maintenance it takes. But I guess if it had been my son I would have done the same.

CHAPTER 14

Getting back to normal

When the treatment was over I re-evaluated my life. I now saw my tumour not as a death sentence, as I had in the beginning, but as an opportunity - an opportunity to do everything I had wanted to do in my life, without waiting, and those who know me well know that I don't like waiting, so this gave me the perfect excuse. I decided to create as many memories as I could so within the space of six months.

The Belgian Grand Prix. Having always wanted to go to a Grand Prix, and having been born in Belgium, this seemed the one to go to. We dragged our neighbours along and had a fabulous time. It was very noisy and I never managed to get any photos of the cars when they were racing, as they were too flipping fast, but I wore my shirt with pride as it was the winner's team (typical me though, I only bought the shirt as I liked it best, not for the team)!

Macmillan cake baking – what a laugh, and what

a mess! The champagne ones were delicious, although maybe we shouldn't have drunk the remaining half bottle of champagne before we had finished baking. It was great to be able to do that to put something back, as Macmillan were heavily involved in my care, but it really took it out of me. I spent the rest of the week resting. They raised over £80 though, which I thought was fantastic.

Ice Bar, London – with a group of our closest friends. It was stunning and the food lovely, but wow it was cold. The special clothing they provided didn't do any good, and they ignored my pleas to be given another coat so I lasted for around 10 minutes before I had to dive into the ladies to use the hand dryer to warm up. Fortunately the food was served downstairs and was delicious – I would recommend people visit, but go prepared. No staying in the Ice Hotel for me!

Christmas and New Year 2011 – I thought it was going to be a quiet Christmas with just my husband and me, so I got the shock of my life when I arrived at my neighbours on Christmas Eve to find my parents there. It was a much better Christmas than the previous year, except that I had couriered their presents to Spain at a cost of around £90 - no wonder my husband had tried to look after them for me!

New Year was a chance for me to celebrate a new

start with a glass of bubbly (or two) and look forward to a happy and healthy New Year with my friends and family.

CHAPTER 15

Getting back to normal

Remember, the diagnosis of a brain tumour is not the end. It is possible to live life to the full. It only stops if you let it. **BE POSITIVE.**

What to expect when you're on chemotherapy:

- Nausea, possibly sickness
- Loss of appetite
- Constipation
- Peripheral neuropathy – tingling in parts of your body, particularly hands, feet and legs
- Joint stiffness
- Skin pain – feels like its tearing when people hold you too tight
- Backache
- Tiredness and fatigue - knees may feel as though they are going from under you, even talking to people can make you tired

- Weepiness
- Loneliness
- Reduced resistance to infections, coughs and colds
- Weight loss
- Weight gain (if on steroids)
- Hair loss (not usually on PCV)
- Weak nails

It's a depressing list – but you can triumph! Here is my advice for coping with a brain tumour and all the problems that go with it:

- Always take your anti-sickness tablets at the time stated – don't deviate.
- Make sure you don't eat anything on the 'forbidden list' – it varies per chemo, so I won't go into that (mine was mainly cheese, alcohol and yeast extract).
- Drink LOTS of water and eat plenty of fruit vegetables.
- If you really can't manage to eat much and your weight drops significantly, talk to your chemotherapy nurse about taking Complan. It is very easy to take, just like a milkshake and full of all the vitamins and nutrients that you need.

- Try to take a walk every day, even if it's only round the block, to get your joints moving.

- Don't be afraid to tell people you are tired or having a bad day. If people visit and you are tired they will understand. Rest is so important and chatting can be exhausting.

- Don't set out to climb mountains. Start with molehills.

- Talk to people. Don't forget you are not alone going through chemotherapy, and if you don't want to upset your family by talking about your fears there are plenty of other people you can talk to. Start with your Macmillan nurse, but it's good to talk to your family.

- Get out and about. Visit friends and let them visit you – just ask them whether they have any little cherubs with bugs before you see them, you don't want to catch anything.

- Be prepared for some friends to appear to have 'ditched' you – some simply cannot handle it, even family members.

- Don't overdo it when you have a good day and feel well. Stop before your legs tell you you have overdone it.

- Put everything on the calendar straight away – a 'chemo brain' often makes you forget things.

- Don't turn help away.

- Get to know your local taxi firm and your bus timetable.

- Have 'me' time – massages, facials, manicures – I looked after my skin all the way through as it can dry out, and I kept my nails painted.

- If you go anywhere for dinner and you are on PCV, take gravy granules with you, as restaurants tend to use gravy with yeast extract in it

- Use a pillow between your legs when sleeping if your skin gets sore.

- Get a nice hot water bottle for backache.

- Buy a simple fleece throw to keep on the settee if you get cold – or simply if you just want some comfort (I still use mine now, as does my cat).

- Keep warm – joints are always worse when they are cold.

- Don't be afraid to have a good old cry. You can't put a brave face on all the time, and it will often help to put things back into perspective.

- Above all, be positive and carry on living your life. 'Down days' are allowed, but dwelling on your problems isn't!

Life today

At first I used to hanker after my old life. I did not really accept that I would never get it all back. I used to want to be able to go shopping for hours, have cocktails in cocktail bars and drink glasses of champagne, sit in the sunshine all day long (with sun cream on obviously), drive my son around and have my independence. I kept hankering for this until two years after the operation when my consultant told me, point blank, that I had to accept that I was never going to get my old life back and I had to start a new one and work round my limitations.

I was devastated. I had to mourn for my old life, and I shed quite a lot of tears. To top it off I was told I would never work again. The only light at the end of the tunnel was that there was hope I might get my driving licence back, but nobody knew when. I had always assumed that I would get my energy back, my headaches would eventually disappear, I would get off my anti-seizure medication and be able to drink more than one glass of alcohol and I would get back to normal. That wasn't going to happen.

After a while I accepted it and made plans in my head to start a new life, as fulfilling as the old. I was still frustrated by being so tired all the time and feeling like an old woman. A friend of mine shed some light on this and told me I wasn't just having physical fatigue, but more to the point, brain fatigue, which I had never heard of.

The chemotherapy makes you weak and tired, but I am a year off chemo now and still suffering. I get so tired that I have to have a sleep most afternoons before Lewis gets home from school. Some days I am fine and have quite a bit of energy, others I can barely get out of bed without it being a great effort; this is brain fatigue. People with brain tumours and the damage from surgery and all the treatments we endure find it more difficult to do 'normal thinking'. Normal people do many things without thinking, but for us even doing a shopping list is a mental marathon. This overstimulation of the brain is why we get tired - our brains need to shut down and reboot. Tthey are fragile!

I now know that if I have an event or trip planned, or even a dinner party, I have to have at least two days' rest to leave me with enough energy to enjoy it. I have now accepted that I will be like this forever. It may get slightly better, but I fear not. I find that total silence allows my brain to rest too, but then that allows my tinnitus to creep in so I can't win!

The hardest times are weekends, when I want to

enjoy time with my family. I love being a mum and a wife but constant socialising all weekend leaves me needing a total rest day on Monday.

I had thought initially that I was depressed, as there were times where I wanted to be alone and didn't want to talk to people. Now I realise that I simply need to give my brain a rest before being ready to socialise again. I can now plan for events and lead a pretty active social life again. My family understand it better now, so they don't question it when I go off for a snooze!

I still have to deal with the after effects of the surgery, radiotherapy and chemotherapy. When I first wake up I am very stiff and have to hold on to the banister when coming down the stairs, so everyone knows it's me. I get more or less daily headaches and frequent migraines, which I never really suffered from before, and I still feel as if I have a tense machine throughout my body in various locations from the peripheral neuropathy. When trying to hold a conversation I often struggle to find the right word when I am tired, and my memory is shot! If I don't get out what I want to say when I think it, its gone. I try not to worry about these though. My dad once told me 'if you can't do anything about it, forget about it'. Wise words. I am still here!

I managed to get my driving licence back and I have

a blue badge which makes it easier, so I can get to Starbucks myself now. I enjoy the odd glass of champagne and cocktails and we do get out and about again (we're back to being cinema goers). All our friends know what we as a family have been through and tend to look after me wherever we go, so I feel comfortable being with all of them. I now fly first class (where possible) on long-haul flights – I have the excuse that the pressure is better and if I see something I really like, I buy it. You can take it with you!

My hair didn't grow back fully from the radiotherapy and is still extremely slow, so I have had a hair system fitted which means I don't have to wear wigs any more, and that is a great feeling. It did a lot for my confidence.

I have plans for fundraising for charities, which I can organise from home, and would like to volunteer at the oncology department at my local hospital as they are so understaffed. I have set up a local brain tumour support group and made some fantastic friends through it.

I would say the biggest change in me is probably the appreciation of my family. I now look after the home (me a housewife - I was a business woman!) I am here when Lewis gets home from school and drive him mad by asking about his day. I think what I love most is being around for my family and doing things for them, creating special memories. I miss my parents a lot more and go out to visit them in Spain more than I used to. Lewis didn't tend to want for a lot before, and he certainly doesn't now.

I have a lot to be thankful for.